1985

Clio's Children

D1546372

ALSO BY JOHN ALLMAN

Walking Four Ways in the Wind

(Princeton University Press, 1979)

Clio's Children

Dostoevsky at Semyonov Square
and other poems

John Allman

A New Directions Book

ACKNOWLEDGMENTS
Grateful acknowledgment is made to the following publications, in which
the poems in this book first appeared: *The Agni Review, The American
Poetry Review, The Massachusetts Review, The Memphis State Review,
New Directions in Prose and Poetry, New Jersey Poetry Journal, Poetry
Northwest, Poetry Now*

"Crazy Horse in 'A Little Flat Place at the Edge of a Few Trees,' " "Roald
Amundsen at the South Pole," "Emma Goldman Deported to Russia," and
"Mohandas Gandhi Awakened by Flashlights near the Sea" were originally
published in *The Chowder Review*.

"Marcus Garvey Arrested at the 125th Street Station" was included in *Push-
cart Prize VIII: The Best of the Small Presses, 1983–84 Edition* (Pushcart
Press), reprinted from *The Agni Review*.

"George Sand at Palaiseau" and "Bruno Bettelheim at Dachau" were written
under the auspices of a Faculty Fellowship in Fine Arts awarded by the
Research Foundation, State University of New York.

Manufactured in the United States of America
First published clothbound and as New Directions Paperbook 590 in 1985
Published simultaneously in Canada by Penguin Books Canada Limited

Library of Congress Cataloging in Publication Data

Allman, John, 1935–
    Clio's children.

    (A New Directions Book)
    I. Title.
PS3551.L46C5   1985   811'.54   84-22659
ISBN 0-8112-0935-0
ISBN 0-8112-0936-9-(pbk.)

New Directions Books are published for James Laughlin
by New Directions Publishing Corporation,
80 Eighth Avenue, New York 10011

to the memories
of my mother and my sister
and Tom Killian

CONTENTS

IV

PREFACE

The personae I use, the moments I represent, indeed this entire book, are based on the following assumptions: that the realities of history are incarnate in human character; that a writer can project himself into the circumstances and personalities of history and express himself in the terms of an historical moment; that a poet can meditate on history itself and convert facts into a type of imagistic consciousness; that the past can be addressed rhetorically and recreated at the same time; that the theme of incarceration present throughout the book is an event that repeats itself in history, authority of the state hemming in always the power or force of the individual; that art is an activity that contravenes and assimilates the dominance-seeking modes of society; that modern life can be framed by events occurring between 1849 and 1945.

In some ways, the collection is a poetic rendering of an idea contained earlier in Thomas Carlyle's *Heroes and Hero Worship,* but the poems here include women, and the title would be more appropriately, *Heroes and Heroines.* I have told no lies for the sake of dramatic heightening, and I have tried to represent all types of personalities, people of amazing gifts, whose greatness is a challenge to our obsessions with the small and quotidian. These are the children of Clio, the muse of history, goddess of renown.—J.A.

I

Dostoevsky at Semyonov Square
1849

It's snowing into the prison courtyard, into the fog,
    into your sleep: bits of light chipping
    off Tatar cheekbones. They're taking you
somewhere. The young soldier, with a wispy red beard
like yours, tells you: "We have been told to tell you
    nothing." You nod. There's Petrashevsky
    and Durov, hunched shadows, temples hollow
as spoons, otherwise unchanged, like specimens in jars
of alcohol. Did they talk? The soldier reminds you of you,
    racing in the woods of Darovoye, between birch
    and hazel trees, naked swords and blue uniforms.
The wart on his cheek. A dull copper button. The beauty
of Russia, vivid as a red glove, the crushed skull
    of a horse,
    General Rostovtsev's teeth: the mind sharpening itself
    on details, as hooves echo off stone walls,
you're pushed forward. Belinsky who put you here was right.
Men traffic in men. Christ wears the Tzar's epaulettes.

But who invented such cold? Thin overcoat, shirt, cravat,
    Yanovsky's borrowed suit: you're fit for an
    interview. Must you always owe 500 roubles?
"Mikhail, I shall be a great success or leap into the Neva."
"All I desire is to keep well." What is the lesson of damp
    straw? A window eight feet high? A metal
    table on which those before you etched
their names? You shiver, and recognize the silence
in the soldier's gray eyes: the five closed silhouettes
    of waiting carriages. ("Driver, to Shill's
    house. Quickly!") In you go, not alone,
four to a carriage, the one window opaque with frost.

You scratch at the light with your unbitten nail
    as the guard
    tells you to stop or he'll be flogged.
    Must you be sympathetic? Poor Grigoriev
is giggling, falling apart in the corner of this last
boxed-in space you'd gladly occupy for a thousand years.

Or is this a dream, the rocking motion of a cradle?
    "Maminka, I am overcome with sadness . . ."
    The driver's whip cracking overhead like God's
knuckle, you have mother's medallion, rubbed smooth,
thumbed beyond recognition, like your first book's extravagant
    praise. A tremor in your groin.
    Father's hopes crushed in the hands
of peasants. How many ways did Belinsky do you in?
"I was wrong about D. He's a hack." You engineer
    your own interrogation, as horizontals
    invade your mind, knee jolts against knee.
At Moscow windows, you saw the patients from the Hospital
of the Poor, brushing past the hedge, their gowns open
    in the back.
    Now if some healer told you to kneel, you'd kneel.
    To go on breathing, you'd kiss
the hand opening the carriage door, as you stoop into freezing
air, gleaming cupolas above you, the Holy Virgin of Vladimir.

There must be 3000 people here, rubbing their hands,
    stamping like the soldiers' horses
    backing into dung. The steam obscuring
their eyes, the breath escaping through the peasants'
crenelated teeth, rising like the clouds above boiling
    cabbage. Your face should be wrapped in
    scarfs like bandages. You see the platform,

a bandstand covered with black cloth, under two inches
of white: the morning turning inside-out, as sun breaks through
    like a dream, like a legend
    of church spires. Oh no one will die.
How wonderful the Tzar is, his angels descending with sabers,
prodding awareness to the pitch of ecstasy. How neat they are,
    three oak posts
    in the ground, perfectly spaced. There's
    Speshnev, Palm, Mombelli, casting parallel
shadows on the snow. You're mounting the hastily built platform
outside yourself, amazed, looking down on your blond head.

Never such fatigue, never such clarity: the church
    burning through the scrim of fog,
    the sunlight like a bishop's upended crook,
glinting near your neck. You're at the far end
of the first row, intrigued by the crumpled edges
    of cloth pulled tight over angles
    and oblong shapes in the cart they're
driving up. How discreetly the driver keeps his
distance. How precisely stacked the coffins are,
    criss-crossed like fingers. Could you breathe
    on the bottom, beneath two layers of friends?
Some of you are being separated out, born noble, brought
forth: the soldier holding the sword over your head
    snaps it mid-
    air, reducing you to an ordinary man.
    Your soul writhes, convulsed, revolted
by the measure of darkness you might have unsheathed
in sour attic rooms, brandishing an axe, or hateful grin.

You kneel, disgraced and penitent, kissing
    the crucifix offered by the priest
    who walks between the rows. Your lips

almost freeze to the metal, like those of dead Jews
in a *shtetl,* face down in the ironworks, purged
   by heavenly Cossacks. Every man bends to it,
   even Petrashevsky, whom they're dressing
in a white, hooded gown, as he laughs: "They
don't know how to dress a man." You have five minutes
   to divide three ways. Farewell to friends
   not yet tied to posts. Greetings to the worn
sinners rising like saints from the gray creases of your
brain, in the harrowing of your past, as you struggle
   to clear the
   strangled vowel of your voice in the mystery
   of being cruel to be wise. How lucky you are.
You'd have gone mad in a wallow of hopes, in a grammar
of lust, beyond the cool hand of the Tzar, uncorrected.

The last minute is for the torn lace of snowflakes
   beginning to fall; the cart horses champing
   their bits; the cupolas like domes of pale fire;
the sound of Kashkin weeping. How should this cease?
It is impossible the dead should not hear the clods
   of earth breaking two inches
   above their eyes. The rigid look
of the soldier's jaw, like the feel of your pen
draft after draft, is the first intention of a character's
   face. But whose? You would have drawn
   the great sinner, raised him above revolt,
dragged him from monasteries to gaming tables, given him
definition. Your mind is fixed on a point that trembles
   like a dust-
   mote within a drop of water
   hung by mysterious force, pulled narrow
to the flats of gravity. Your feet are suddenly heavy,
your hands wet with light. Could you rise through that sky?

Who is this galloping into the Square, waving a white
   handkerchief? You are saved. Rostovtsev
   grins. The fabled messenger has arrived
in the nick of last minutes: his mustache dryly
pasted above his lip; he is almost too late, descending
   from nowhere, his cloak hanging like
   cardboard drapery, his arms at his sides,
folded wings. Rostovtsev reads your reprieve, stuttering
through the awkward consonants you never thought to hear
   alive. But what is he announcing?
   Four years? Can the heart pronounce it?
You'll be taken to Tobolsk, to Omsk, across the salutary
waste of Siberia, deep into legendary cold, where milk
   spills in thin
   frozen slabs and despair is common as the hard
   muds of April. You do not expect to die again
in a single fetid room, hemmed in by suffering of other men
dour in brimless caps, as you invent your sin and redemption.

Frederick Douglass Waiting for News of the Emancipation Proclamation

1863

The snow will never be
so perfect again, blue in the dusk,
his weariness lit by candles in windows: not the slave's
heavy footfall here in Boston, on the way to Tremont Temple,
where messengers line up,
hand touching hand, Lincoln's pulse
already entering a telegrapher's wrist; the quick chattering
like the shaking of a boy's bones, the nights he can still feel
a ragged shirt between his skin
and nothing, the wind carrying dust
into his stomach. Was there a master who didn't penetrate a black
man's blood? He's poured liquid brass, plucked splinters of ships
he helped launch, given wages
into the white fist broken tonight.
No craftsmen at Chickasaw Bluffs, fallen in the waters of Bull Run,
open-mouthed in peach blossoms at Shiloh. Now they kill each other,
lean as whips, like field workers
torn from families; graves unmarked in swamps.

How many amens fill
a hall? His throat is beginning
to constrict. Fourth to speak, he won't need to avoid
bad eggs, sacks of cayenne pepper, snuff thrown in the eyes.
They're all his own, spread
out beneath the podium; a dark plain
a man can run toward; all these backs that felt a lash. No fleeing
north into Canada. Heads turn as he enters. He'd felt more visible
escaping through Havre de Grace,
a sailor's papers crackling in his pocket.

He's a man of substance! Little Annie spoke to him, last night:
her soul unshackled, thin voice rising like smoke into his hearing,
    but no one leaping into his arms.
    Do daughters die, because fathers hide
in England? America hanged John Brown; ignored *him*, his bulk
and eloquence, pages in *The North Star,* hands that could strangle.
    "Without the shedding of blood,
    there is no remission of sin."

    Seated onstage, should he
    stand to this applause? Dear Anna,
at home, couldn't decipher a sentence; knew the press of his body,
children surging out of her; scowled in a corner, beyond words,
    nodding at his preacher's
    intonations. What could he tell her now?
Their children will be accepted at school? His white Julia was only
a friend who could read? He gets up, behind Martin, Dickinson,
    keeping the crowd calm,
    his gray-streaked head
lifted like a lion's. He's the man who broke the man-breaker,
who was beaten senseless in shipyards, too literate for a slave.
    He's hoarse from shouting.
    Are there words to snap an iron
link? In the wire's hum, the beginning of song? His chest swells.
Muscles in his legs awaken. Someone's yelling, It's here, It's here.
    A thaw
    in northern rivers; a breaking loose.

George Sand at Palaiseau
1865

August

For the moment, no bad odor. Limbs bend. Eyes stare
      toward the memory of the hand
closing them. She washes him quickly, changes
his nightgown; plants flowers between the rim of his body
      and August air,
      faithful Alexandre.
He'd said nothing when she ran off with Marchal.
How he whimpered in the cold bath, telling her
      to continue Fuster's
      treatment, saddened
by the burden he was for Madame. Fifteen years,
still he would not use *tu*. Did she ever love a man
      not frail? His hand
      thin as light, lifting
a gesture to the window, sliding beyond her grasp.
Wheat fields, bloodied by sun, streaming toward Paris.

Without him, now, she will write . . . advice to new friends.
      Flaubert would redo the scene,
rearrange the pillows, have a cart rumble
into a rut, put the window on the west wall,
      lamplight falling obliquely
      on a youthful face.
She listens to birds. The cook's clatter. Downstairs,
last week, his sister held her ears, while he inhaled
      the *gaz*. She remembers
      Valdemosa; Chopin's pallid

hand fading into Études, while she wrote furiously,
her study a *fumoir;* workmen shaking their heads
          after hauling the piano
          up the mountain;
the smell of fish, olive oil, garlic oozing
like salt from the walls, from a thrashing sea.

She's finished the novel, *Le Bonheur,* left intact
          the bits of dialogue Alexandre
contrived. *Their* novel, to give him something
of life, in making art. She reads her diary entry:
          "The will to heal
          is all." Not the oaf
her son, Maurice, called him, he seems perfectly
quiet. He'd won some of the arguments, rewritten
          some of the parts
          for the puppet shows
at Nohant. And she sewed clothes, the tiny
trousers, while friends argued across the room
          with the dancing
          marionettes. A son's jealousy
swells like the Indre, swirls a muddy water
about her thighs. Lovers are swept away like debris.

Men say she talks like a man, the odor of cigars
          in her hair,
clinging to her dress, the stink of equality.
What a husband forgets a son picks up as his own:
          Maurice, imminent
          landlord of Nohant, seigneur
of orchards, pavilion, and woods, telling her she's
too old. For two nights, she sits near the body,
          mourning little Nini
          and Cocoton, the grandchildren

also gone. The cupboard of her hearing about to close,
how long will she write of love? Visitors arrive, but
        not upstairs: his sister weeping,
            fearing the dead face. The church will not
bless his ground. She must carry him into plain earth.
"Do not worry. I shall not be ill. I refuse to be ill."

November

In the morning, autumn glistens. Alexandre's presence,
        as in life, recedes, allowing her
to be herself. It was good to be in Paris, the Odéon,
Théâtre-Français, where the voice carries out of Nature
        the passion life cannot
            afford. Perhaps she'll write
Marchal; tell how blood rises, old women clutch
their shawls, remembering the long hands of Liszt.
        Her mood is for children's
            tales. At night, crisp
emanations of the stars. Recently, at dawn, mist
rolling through trees, fluency returned: ten pages,
        and birds
            flapping into the wet air.
She emerges from the cloud of cigarette smoke, someone's
Muse, but does not find him etching, dark eyes dilating.

Marchal, fat darling, this morning in Paris, an early
        breakfast, someone else
in your arms, what do you remember of art?
It's a new age, seeking hardness; Flaubert's music
        of objects.
            Poor Marie, beloved Dorval,
that full voice breaking over an audience of stones.
"Dear Gustave, what are you doing?—grinding away,

I fancy, you, in solitude too. . .
   mother probably in Rouen. Do you
sometimes spare a thought for 'the old troubadour
of the ale-house clock, who sings, and will always sing
    of perfect love'?"
   The wind creaks toward winter,
sweeping voices aloft, an opera of the damned. Someone will
write of her. The peasants of La Châtre? A drunken mayor?

No one believes in her minor aches—as if she owned
    more than her reputation,
with Solange, her daughter, the slut of Europe!
The lead weight of the Second Empire still keeps wives
    in place. Let the lovers
    enter their fiacres,
drive south away from husbands who tattle in books
about nothing. In old age, a new magnetism: the moon
    drawing up the vapors
    of a ragged field,
pulling at her blood, tugging the half-surfaced soul
that keeps going under. In abstinence, a red death.
    Marchal, huge springtime,
    we grow plump, and France
lacks exaltation. How many dinners purchase a hug?
I'm an infant, without sex or energy, blinking at the dark.

She pulls at her hair, remembering how she'd cut it off
    and sent it in a box
to Musset, a final blow. Poor Alfred, on the crossing
to Genoa, groaning in his cabin, sick as a girl.
    She wrote for hours,
    stood on deck, took sea-spray
full in the eyes. Delacroix would paint her now
all lines, without color: changing his art

        because she did not
        remain young.
She can still look to heaven! Hands clasped, face
pale in its own light. She can still hear Balzac
        huffing up the stairs,
        hugging loaves of bread
for Jules and the runaway Aurore. She hears mice. A faint
scratching at her heart. Things from God that must return.

Crazy Horse in "A Little Flat Place at the Edge of a Few Trees"

1874

Your woman has the coughing sickness. Meat racks hang
        downwind of nothing.
        Lodges are torn open
like a warrior's stomach. The helpless ones are thin
as the scent of water in the moon of new grass.
        You are here
        from sun to sun.
No spirit carries a stone from the world beyond this one,
crashing through the forest, leaping over your daughter's
        scaffold
        where you lie
next to her bundled body. No lightning divides the tree.
Not even the hands of enemies pull you away
        as light falls
        like worms from Agency flour
and songs of Pa Sapa become dust in the people's mouth.
Was she truly They Are Afraid of Her when no one fears you?

There is nothing to bring back from this place for the people.
        Hunger makes your face small,
        the scar from No Water's bullet
tightens above your lip. You count coup on the bodies
of air. The old way of fighting is good for the pictures
        on someone else's shirt.
        Old wounds do not bring
Little Hawk or Hump, brother, teacher, lifting
the lodge flap, entering smoke. Night summons them
        to the darkness of Crow
        and Pawnee, their ghosts

walking with new limps, Loafers wearing white man's pants,
their death songs lost in the wind. Your daughter does not hear
      you. Her bones whiten
      in the red blanket
for Wolf. You address the birds who come to carry off
what there is of her. Your voice flutters, caught on a branch.

What good was it your father gave you his name?
      Holy Man,
      long ago:
taking no scalps, riding the horse from which only your people
can throw you, the red-back hawk tied to your head, your hair
      free, the lightning
      jagged on your cheek,
your skin light as the moon of new calves. You feel coldness
in anger. You kill the white man. The Crow. The bad-smelling
      soldier scouts. But there is
      not enough powder
to carry bullets where they must go, into the hearts of Blue
Water and Sand Creek, into the hunger of the white man's
      sweet lumps and moldy
      bacon, into Black Buffalo Woman's
smile. Blood freezes in the wound. No skewers of a Sun Dance
made a twisting like this. You are lowest of Hunkpatila.

It is time to leave her. Even the light stiffens in trees.
      The emptiness she departs
      is the place within you
where the hand does not reach, where skin pulls taut
and cracks. You close your eyes and see the dust rising
      from the plains, the wagon guns
      jolting out of ruts
where the buffalo wallowed. The breath-clouds
of Oglala ponies will be the fog through which no one

returns. The people walk,
like the old times. They don't
find relatives, sleeping robes, the river that never ends.
What can you give them but a way to die. You climb down
the tree. Something rushes
through the leaves,
snorting. You run back. You tell the people nothing.
You listen to coughing and stare into the fire.

II

William Morris Boating up the Thames
to Kelmscott Manor
1880

You name this rented houseboat
The Ark, going upriver, through locks and weirs,
where men pile August hay on punts, the corn-crake cries in grasslands,
rooks scream in elms. That's the odor of lime. It's almost a day
  to forget the unemployed, police batons,
  sooty faces; sun setting this water ablaze,
while retired colonels, reading *The Times,* hoot from armchairs, praise
horses riding into uplifted hands. Jane's in the cabin, fighting off
  asthma: the black fog in her lungs, your
  proximity. She never enjoyed a broad body,
woodworker's hands. Long and pallid, Rossetti's dream in blue
silk: she's full-length, free now of pain in her back; black hair
  descending in waves, hands folded, Dante's
  wife jailed above the marshes of Maremma.
You, and daughters, and friends, towed by Biffen's men: goggle-eyed
drunk; another, too thin. They hook you onto a mercantile tin kettle,
  your bow slapping all the way to
  Twickenham, spray in your beard.

Tea above Kingston: color
  imprinted like fingers burning through
the sky; your mind, streaked by Northern Lights, twisting
toward Thorshaven, crags of Iceland, wasted slopes, the happiest
  struggle in the face of death. Jane pours.
  DeMorgan calls you an imposter. You get another
tow, after dismissing Biffen's men. You haven't touched an oar yet.
The girls clap. You'll cook for everyone! Men should live with plain
  floors, whitewashed walls. Oh let them
  scrape Oxford smooth, obliterate a rough-hewn

joy. No future's clean. Jane tucks away the letter from Rossetti,
words heavier than that barge of bricks; hands cool. Oh you'll cook!
      In Moulsey Lock, waiting for the water
        to raise *The Ark*, gates to swing open,
you drop the candle from the lamp, a spring slips, light hisses out.
"By damn!" Jane blinks. Here, there's no window to throw dinner
        out of. You won't
        kick a rented door into the Thames.

      You and Price sleep in *The Ark*,
        the hot night, swaying. The ladies and Dick
and DeMorgan hold their noses at the Magpie Inn, try the foul
beds. You listen to toads and crickets. The boat, rising
        on the tide's inhalation, begins to move
        away from the mooring, away from the simple
loops of quick hands. (You know where this water flows: river
before the maelstrom epileptics dream of, falling off to nowhere.
        Jenny's twitching in her bed, frail
        daughter.) How beautiful she was, Jane
in repose, your Guenevere; the cup you brought her, a muted gleaming,
as in tapestries the wealthy pay you to hang on their walls. What
        does man leave but the memory of
        labor? It's morning: sky fleeing westward,
your line in the water. One gudgeon. A small dace. They gasp
in your world. You watch the knot of swallows overhead, in pursuit,
        opening like a bag of needles above the hawk,
        chasing him toward Eaton Hastings.

      Everyone's back on board by 10:00.
        Another lock. A long tow to Windsor Bridge.
The day effortless and languid as the look of Burne-Jones'
women, though you bark your shins, wasps find you hove to.
        The air quick, whimsical, you're in the cabin,
        cooking on the spirit-lamp, DeMorgan outside,
swatting. The girls run along the bank, falling into high grass.

(No savage workers here, blackened faces rising like apparitions
      in northern smoke.) Sunset!
        Even Jane laughs, going ashore, buttoning
the top of her dress, while haze settles on the river's throat.
Good lodging at Bridge Hotel: beds clean, empty as space in warps;
      the women in one room, giggling;
      the men here, snoring like Biffen's drunk.
(At Hammersmith, upstairs, you wanted only reasonable labor,
reasonable rest: solace of the loom at dawn, rattling the shuttle
      back and forth; Jane under the covers,
      stopping her ears, while you shook the room

        with patterns of daisy, wild grape,
      papered the walls with vegetables, fruit, above a street's
torn cry, unmended lung). You can't sleep in such noise, thinking
of Iceland's hummocks. Lava fields. Nakedness of glaciers, massive
      capes slipping from bony
      shoulders; all that white collapsing in sun,
into Rossetti's hands. You stare at the wall's scarlet flock;
flowers fading in dampness. DeMorgan's on his back, stertorous,
      shattering the air; the river hidden;
      not even merlins flying in thick mist,
your eyes wet, fingers itching. There's no tool to shape this mood.
A good day to see Eton! You buy bread, and Price discovers
      a cucumber thick as a boy's
      arm. You're fine, afloat, until Bray Lock:
your foot throbs, goutish, tender, as if gripped too long; Jane's
wincing, blood rushing from her face into the twisting of her
      spine. DeMorgan shouts.
      Too late. The Ark drifts into a pair of barges,

        the starboard door splinters
      like a thin wall. You can smell the cargo
of green timber. Price falls into a mock faint. You trade
epithets with the captain, steer off, shaking your fist. May

writes in your diary:
        "a mountain before a plain . . .
a dust heap before a gentleman's house." At last, chalk
slopes falling away, past Cookham. You've avoided another
        tin kettle. (Is there a way to change
        course? You decorate palace walls. Empire swells
to engulf Afghanistan, for a "scientific frontier," lashes out
at Kaffirs, the Zulus. Gladstone's homily is of tragic ends. No
        use in your painted thistle.)
        Tonight, you sleep in *The Ark,*
on the flood, while Jane curls up at the Inn. Aurora Borealis:
light splits open; the moon dissolves. In Iceland, nothing so green
        as this day, or quick
        as the silvery bleak huddled at your line.

        Next morning, it's Lady Place
        and Margrave. The women watch two men
splashing naked in the river. "They're looking for Moses
in the rushes." Even Jane titters. Suddenly, there's a line
        of poor children at water's edge
        whining, begging for coppers. Anger
explodes in your hand waving them away. You damn the accident
of birth that put them there; you, here. But you reach Oxford:
        Salter's mooring. Charles will meet everyone
        at Radcot, lifting the lantern as you disembark,
voices drifting toward the shadows of polled trees. High up and safe
in Kelmscott, Jane will open Rossetti's letters. You'll sigh,
        solicitous about his health; she'll lie down beneath
        his drawings from Dante, another headache coming on.
Is that a blue titmouse? They've not returned with weed sparrows,
pigeon hawks, rooks filling the trees. There's a moorhen; a Cotswold
        look to that house, before they blind
        the birds with zinc roofs. You have things to do!

Books to open. A worker unfolds
    his fabrics, lifts swollen hands from the vat
like a drone made beautiful by indigo. Charles swings the lantern,
laughs. Women tumble onto the dock, dresses wet along the hem,
        your hands hardened by rope and oar,
    face a deeper red, hair wild. You open the door
in the garden wall. It's home: tapestries, stony spaces between;
stairs twisting in the grain of oak trees, split to a knot; leaded
        windows not rattling to heavy feet.
    Jane's lying down. The girls are yawning.
You can't sit still. Rossetti shivered here, complained of dampness
from the Thames, Jane brushing her hair, while you talked of Burne-
        Jones: problems of painting women,
    downcast eyes, profit in craft.
You'll limn no more nymph or faun, lurid leaps across a lord's
cabinet; Jane sitting up, pale, a sculpted Echo. Upriver, you hear
        workers cough blood in shadows of iron
    railings, see the sun fail in dusty gardens.

Anna O
1880–82

"From December 1880 to June 1882 Breuer treated what has become recognized as a classical case of hysteria, that of Frl. Anna O. . . . her name . . . Bertha Pappenheim, deserves to be commemorated."

Ernest Jones, *The Life and Work of Sigmund Freud*

Can she open her throat? His hand smells of chloral,
      plunges in, like the girls
      who drown in Vienna's canal.
On a muddy bottom where no one moves, he sticks a dead needle
in a dead arm. Is that the governess's poodle, lapping
      water from his
      hand? She can't hold the orange.
It rolls toward him, off the bed, onto the floor, gleaming
in the sunlight like his beard, like the goblets in the cabinet,
      a summer
      house
on fire. She squints everything into gray, taffeta
drapes, the rustle of his thighs. Outside, on cobbles,
      the snap of whips,
      Papa sitting behind Talmud
and beard, heavy in his carriage, riding the Ringstrasse,
the circle of his wealth. Herr Doktor, no one ever dies.

And summer has its own musicians in a field, crackling
      a song, as the night train
      pierces the air. When was it
anyone with a family was happy? If she could walk, she'd
rub legs like a cricket, kick off blankets, run out

in last year's brown dress
turning green
with grass stains. Papa gasping on the pillow. Dead.
Really dead. She couldn't help him to the toilet, heal
a lung,
cough like a son.
If she could talk, she'd tell Papa how to run back,
flee the burning pit. She'd call the black dog
wetting her leg
Liebe. If she had
a life of her own, she'd walk through Aunt's gold-frame
mirror, where the skull turns away, combing her hair.

She screams all morning. The healer doesn't come.
He doesn't spoon
his way through the words
that block her speech. Let his friend inject her
for the sake of sleep. Let him blow cigar smoke in her face,
the mind's fog,
while the blind thing
beats in her womb, kicks her side, claws to get out
and cries, falling backward in space. That's him
running away. Men
who touch her
always take feeling with them. The squint returns,
deafness like a door opening and closing, the arm
limp as a snake. Something
crowds her tongue.
Someone pulls down the skin beneath her eyes. She sees him
through a curtain of blood, the androgyne, without muscle.

Nothing sings like sleep. Nothing betrays like talk:
white confessions
carried in his black satchel,

dragged through Vienna's streets, public as Franz Josef's
court. She hears the coachman snoring in a cup, snuffling
     like a chaperon, asleep between
     daughter and father
who take in the Prater's green-tipped trees and sweet air.
The horses are smooth, draped with lilac. Last night,
     she freed a white bird
     trapped in a tree, she danced
alone, blooming in a swirl, running through the garden
between statues of men. When she woke, she was glad
     a white bird came near,
     that Papa doesn't suffer where he is.
In the world without men, her fear falls from everything,
fruit tumbles off the table, her fingers unfold to the sun.

The Wright Brothers at Kill Devil Hills
1903

The wind's pulse, quick
as a sparrow's, tilts whatever wings its way,
that gull skimming the heads of dunes, hills whittled to plateaus.
Three times riding a thin strip of beach, they've squealed along
the wooden track, almost risen
on billows, nosed back to the height
of mammals, the *Flyer's* broken skid leaving skewed prints,
someone limping in the sand. Starched collars. Ties. Suits.
They're crisp as grocery
clerks: Orville twisting
the ends of his mustache, cap fastened with safety pins;
Wilbur straight-lipped, face calm where the sea leaps, mind
wheeling among rafters
in the sky. He's not tired enough
for Dayton, the bicycle shop. Here come Daniels, Dough, Brinkley,
the boy from Nags Head: someone to watch this December hen hawk,
stiff bird's claw
that opens to drop its prey,

ice yet spinning
on the surface of pools, the shed
leaning into drifts, fire guttering in a tin-can stove.
No one steals the wind. Indians once crouched behind tufted
mounds, the rim of Albemarle
Sound; geese paused, honked wildly,
abrupt hands breaking their wings to another need. And Langley's
Aerodrome, four lifters pulling wrong ways, has plunged from its
tower, hissed
into the Potomac. Orville's

hauling with the others, struts imprinting his palm, light slipping
north. The engine sputters and the boy's dog runs; magneto spinning
        sporadic fire. Wilbur's smile fixed,
        false teeth precise; the shinny club
that once broke a boy's speech now the propeller twirling
behind him, as he listens to the language of spiraling currents,
        blood hurtling
        like an arrow thudding into a door.

        He's snug in the hip
        cradle; insinuated angel
on the lower wing; tugging wires that flap a rudder,
twist a roadway in the air. He's waving; let go; scraping
        free of the track, lifting with
        gulls warping their way through gray
gaps of wall no one can see. On his belly, head first, without
helmet, goggles, jodhpurs, only eyelids to deflect the blowing sand,
        he plunges,
        jolts, recovers rolling on ruts
even birds tumble in, frame creaking like Orville's kitchen chair,
the forward elevator, his extra wing, sliding on the curve Lillienthal
        lost, gliding toward Berlin:
        the horizon feathered, these whitecaps
blooming everywhere off Cape Hatteras, as he gathers all shadow
beneath his arms, churning the clouds toward Kitty Hawk, Manteo,
        man with waxen features
        who will not melt though level with the sun.

Roald Amundsen at the South Pole
1911

On the Great
Barrier, one man
up front, on skis, pressing into silence
and fog: sledges behind, dogs howling, whipped
down the steep
curve
of the world, where seas meet to end every
direction. You're not racing Scott for the Pole,
you say in
diaries. Good policy
to lighten sledges to the weight of feathers,
heating oil, matches. The hollow hummocks
sift
into a crevasse,
astounding falling away of the two halves of noise,
and no shadow falls, not even the hairline
of a false
horizon,

no instinct
measures
how instruments freeze. You remember
Lindstrom's hotcakes. The flow of syrup.
Do you have
the heart for
this? Somewhere west, Scott's ponies
being slaughtered for the final blizzard,
and in your
tent, breath

turning to crystal. You leave snow-beacons,
white cairns with blubber and biscuits
                    all the way
                    from the Ross Sea
to the Heiberg Glacier. After the mountains,
        fewer dogs. The quickness of Wistig's
                    rifle. Faithful
                    blood streaming

                    downhill, freezing
                    to survivors
who howl with hunger, like yourself: dog filets
boiled with vegetable pemmican, while you scribble
                    notes, remember
                    April, the sun's
last witness, when it disappeared six months
lost below a solid sea. Killing. Much killing
                    The Bay
                    curving red
with Adélie penguins, crab-eater seals (first
photographed), skua gulls. Anything that came
                    to watch,
                    sacrificed,
eaten. Months from now, navigating the *Fram*,
        the skin of your cheeks a new pink,
                    though
                    here the frost-sores

                    harden in the time
                    between yawning
and shivering, you'll stamp your foot
to feel it drive against planks, your native
                    trees,
                    remembering how ice

calves off the land-mass into bergs. The wind's
up. Pitch of howls higher than the wind. You
                walk where no one
                ought to be,
no one can stay, leaving a note to King Haakon
in the Polar tent, for delivery by Scott, Norway's
                flag. He'll
                find everything
in place, except his return: while you plunge
    back to where the Barrier begins, man of
                method, lashing
                bony backs and haunches.

D. W. Griffith Filming *The Birth of a Nation*
1914

Doors open through a flat world
into weeds; hammers knocking; the post-bellum South
rising on Sunset's westward curve: tintype father in collar
and tie, legs crossed, he tells Bixter to separate white sheets
strung on the line, let in
more sun; the roofless set open to sky,
dust of unpaved roads; indoor actors filmed in a sheen, as if
lifting their faces to the moon, resurrecting the Carolina
state house. A blackface
speaker on the dais bangs his gavel;
white citizens cringe in the gallery; a senator eats fried chicken,
looks over his shoulder into Bixter's Pathé, the camera punching
sprocket-holes, bogus Negroes draining
whiskey from bottles of tea. It's the black tide,
the scalawag ruination: his boyhood poverty on the farm in
Floydsburg; daddy, Colonel Jake's feet up on the porch rail, bourbon
staining the air, while he sits in the shadow
of that great voice, hears of the charge

against Union troops. He's
the patriarch here; his voice booming
above the clatter of Bixter's camera moving in on the feigned
ruckus of politicians. Why did the family flee to Louisville,
the Colonel die? He wants more back-slapping,
flailing of arms, minstrel-show
grinning. A straw hat keeps sun off his shaved head; tanned
patches on his skull from holes punched in the crown for air,
like discs of darker
skin. There's Miss Gish,

the ethereal Biograph saint he once filmed ascending to heaven,
sun streaming through a halo of blonde hair. Does he need her
       yet? He dances out of his
       chair; bows; leads her into the shade;
sings something from *Tosca*; bows; suddenly begins boxing shadows,
transparent partners on the wall, his reflexes quick. The real thing
       is lunch; water at $2 a barrel; the mirror
       that Bix flashes on a wounded Lincoln

       and the Pathé swings too high,
    films the Hollywood Hills above the wall.
It's a noble truth the people crave, he thinks, in the clearing
where one-armed Wilson's empty bombs blow sawdust and lampblack
       into the dry bed of the Los Angeles
       River. The South's final battle in mock
Petersburg: muskets rented from Bannerman's shoot paraffin wads,
spray into the wind. The extras in Goldstein's uniforms are still
       unshaven, animal-ripe
       from weeks on skid-row. They'll do
to keel over in the Union bombardment, shirts open, exposing
pasted-on wounds. He waves his hat at Von Stroheim, bald head
       amid so much blue. The smoke rolls behind,
       the attack begins backward,
rear lines moving on those in front, every man falling to friendly
fire, trees exploding behind stone walls, while he finds no focus
       among ex-Negroes: smudges
       from last scene's hilarity

       like deliberate dirt
     under riflemen's eyes, like war paint on real
Indians he filmed in Cuddebackville, in the Orange Mountains,
at Neversink River. An actor holds up a bloodied hand, complains
       he has to defend himself.
       Clouds pour from pots under trees.

The Little Colonel rouses men from trenches, leads the charge
with hops-pickers unemployed only yesterday, now slumping forward,
        twisted on their arms, a fog
            enveloping them like gas, death a kind of job
when all else fails. Not Germans smashing through Liege, Namur,
closing the noose around France: men much aggrieved, rushing onto
        bayonets, into the crouching Bixter's
        Pathé. "That's good, that's good!"
Raw negative rushed to the lab, thin as living membrane; Karl Brown,
in the Mazda glare, filming white titles on a black background.
        Darkness comes out gray; letters
        like ante-bellum cotton in Caucasian hands.

        He's thirsty; bruised;
    Charlie's open Packard straining upward
on a service road; small landslides, crumbs from a lizard's
mouth. He sits facing backward on the folded top, looking down
        the mountain, the way twisting
            inside the cracked bed of another lost
river. It's not history he frames here, between desiccated borders,
not the unrecorded voice of slave women in billowing dresses: no
        runagate man surviving swamps
        ever came this high, or children
sold across a county, sister in the shack, beneath the master,
eyes rolling. Can he strike the ground, fill these ruts with water,
        create streams for hooded horsemen
        to plunge through, into the audience's lap?
Brown, in the front seat, cradles the Pathé, craning his neck
as they lurch onto something straight, almost smooth, the road
        passing the Patton insane
        asylum. "Want to get out here?" Bixter laughs.

        Suddenly, the Packard's grinding
    in a slash between exposed roots, the clutch
smoking. Charlie crawls under; dusts the leather facing

slick with heat; talcum rising in clouds, his tanned face
              emerging white, broken
              by a grin. Light slants over the dam,
Big Bear Lake, finger's width of road between drowning
and falling back down into the valley among grapevines
              coated with sand.
              Who created this place?
What air! It's paying off: running, twirling Indian clubs;
sparring his way into stamina. He's got alimony to pay, another South
              to build, a woman leaping
              off these rocks for her virtue.
He's the same man who slept on freights back to Louisville,
his shoes tied up in rags. Bixter says the Pathé will be cool
              at this height; static electricity
              will scratch the film, scar an actor's face.

              Too much sun. It's dance
          he wants: Little Sister, the white girl hardly
touching the ground, fluttering on the path through silence;
Gus, blackface trooper, pursuing her, running upright, his mouth
          foaming with peroxide. He opens his arms
          to embrace a small bird, stumbles between majestic
trees; adjured to stay low, low, bend low, Negro with pale patches
behind his ears, trying to run like a salamander, talcumed joints
          sliding over rocks,
          hands pinching the light that floods
down. The megaphone barks: "as if you mean no harm but can't
help yourself!" He's doubled over, out of breath, spine curving
          to an idea, a whip licking at his
          groin, eyes moving rapidly in the nightmare of
dirt farmers who wake in the middle of the night, losing their women
to whatever ruins crops, burns stables, strips a man's shirt from his
          back. Little Sister is skittering
          left and right, like a wounded quail.

Gus looks at the sky; seems
about to burst into song. "Good. Do it now!"
Little Sister leaps; should drift down like a feather, ride the wind,
glide back home a faithful soul. She plummets; bounces. It's Brown,
letting go a costumed dummy,
almost going over with it, live man clinging
to tree limbs. It's the right person dying in Little Colonel's arms.
Gus straightens up; antiseptic mouth open and pink in a burnt-cork
blackened face.
"Everybody to the meadow!" New straw hat on,
he wants the love scene there, white hands clasped, the man and woman
embracing where linen flowers bloom, the hospital pallor of their
cheeks now
colored by a sudden rush
of blood. They'll soon be weeping in the dusty street of Piedmont.
Who'll pay for Little Sister? The carpet-baggers, the mulatto woman
with her bare shoulder, the African face
that strayed sullenly across the picture,

scenes ago, have all
disappeared, like names suffocated
in excrement of the middle passage; like the clang of trolleys
outside a dark auditorium. He's back in Charlie's Packard, descending
the beautiful
new road they hadn't known of
on the way up. He wants the cowboy extras ready; a stream rerouted;
horsemen in white sheets, white hoods with tall spikes like unicorns
or the Kaiser's men; horses
caparisoned, sweat-stained, eyes wild
in their masks. He wants the land imprinted with a burning cross.
Men in blackface being shot at, doing a dance, dropping dead: he'll
sweep away more of the enemy
than Colonel Jake in the whiskey haze

on his porch. The negative he slides between thumb and forefinger
will yank a world into the light; whip riders rushing to rescue an
audience from
the darkness they never could abide.

Marcel Proust Leaving Princesse
Soutzo's Room at the Ritz

1917

The air, at last: rings deepening around your eyes,
        spilling outward. Who said
        you looked like yesterday's
gardenia? You can hear them droning near the Eiffel
Tower, in the searchlights: German aircraft, Gothas.
        Young Agostinelli
        whom you loved
would be in flames tonight, if he hadn't crashed at sea.
You wonder how much Nembutal to take. Should you ask
        the Abbé Mugnier for a talk?
        The cork walls of your bedroom
begin to crack. Not noise: time itself seeping through,
blown down the Boulevard like asthma powders, your white
        face the mirror
        of empty
pages, while here, so high up, men like Nijinsky
do their death-leaps, horizontal, to no applause.

At the Hôtel Marigny, you ask the butcher's boy
        to describe
        the feel of blood
to the elbow. You pay him and Le Cuziat to pierce
something helpless with hatpins, abuse mother's photo:
        paths to pleasure
        finally without sex,
the unfurling of pain like a black bandage
in your hands in sunlight, *Maman* slipping back
        into her
        dim hallway.

You think of Agostinelli's ghost, how sad he looks
in his black rubber cape, strapped helmet, the "nun
            of speed."
            What noise!
There's one! Spiraling down, a saint's vehicle
flaming in the dawn like a stained-glass window.

Who survives? You remember Yturri, Montesquiou's
            lover, serving
            brandy while you
inhaled the rotten apples of his diabetic breath.
This afternoon, hidden from sun, you'll need more
            caffeine, and when
            Celeste
brings coffee, croissants, you'll tell how Delagarde
hypnotized Beaumont at the Princesse's, how you stuck
            pins
            in his unfeeling
hand, and sirens announced the Germans, and Cocteau
made a joke. Outside, on the balcony, you watched
            the sky
            while women
clutched their pearls, fled in nightgowns,
fighters climbed to the stars, a world fell away.

Manuscripts wobble in their unfinished columns.
            Crumbs
            roll on the bed.
Books collapse around you. You know everyone's
end. Whom do you despise? Kisses withdrawn
            do not always
            linger on the cheek.
Let Le Cuziat keep your dead parents' furniture,
where boys lounge, where mothers do not brush

          hair
          from their eyes.
Some faces go blank before dawn. You cannot
bribe headwaiters for air. The body drains
          into a gesture,
          an intonation,
something remembered. Pressure in your chest: style
flowing like acid from the empty organ of love.

III

Emma Goldman Deported to Russia
1919

Even on Ellis Island, they split darkness before dawn:
    key scraping in the lock; two guards.
"Get Ready." Ethel drops everything, trying to stuff clothes
into a bag. Can such girls be enemies of the state? The male
    deportees huddle in the corridor, one on crutches,
    another carried from his bed, ulcer bleeding
quietly. Berkman, your Sasha, is counting men into groups,
arranging for last telegrams, telephone calls. The inspectors
    say there will be time. But there isn't.
    A brooch holds together the top of your dress,
like a butterfly trapping warmth. You walk between the railings
of the Reception Center, the high hall, where wives from Poland
    lined up for physicals, eyelids lifted
    for signs of trachoma, sick ones marked on the sleeve
with chalk. Palmer and Hoover, physicians of the state, oh they've
x'd you here, winter's coat too short, one's soul showing through
    like a long wrist. The wind rattles windows
    in four towers, howls through arches, stirring snow

into a mist, moonlight glancing off the brooch into the eyes
    of officials. Can they see sedition
inside tin trunks? A thin deportee is weeping, pulling
his portmanteau, avoiding feet. The man in extra coats
    cannot bend to snatch the orange
    rolling across the sanded floor.
"Line up!" It's Caminetti, his uniformed boys. Outside,
deep whiteness; wind almost breaking your grip; armed men
    lining the way, tight-lipped and gray
    as the barge at anchor, that shadow heaving

toward the skyline you cannot see. Are you leaving for Hades?
Grunts. Threats of beatings, A man pushed to the frozen dock.
    Someone blows a whistle all the way
      to Bedloe's Island, and women cross the gangplank,
no heavy coats trailing. Ethel's pulling away from the young
soldier, your footsteps firm, resounding, as he calls after her,
    "I'm sorry!" You hear Sasha telling men
      to keep their bundles taut, hide their money.

The cabin thick with heat; iron stove crackling its innards
    like nutshells. No water. No air. The city
in the porthole, shrinking: Thirteenth Street, Union Square,
half your friends put away. The opaque film evaporates from your
    glasses; sweat trickling into the folds
      of your neck; stains spreading like an eclipse
under each arm. The girls shake free their hair, all this wonder
you once had; full bosom; the high lyric of your voice broken
    by nightsticks. What did you accomplish,
      passing beneath the torch of that woman,
her eyes bleeding toward the sea? You feel the world wobble
on its axis. You hear Sasha arguing. Everyone's buttoning up.
    You're outside, climbing stairs up a rusted
      wall, the decrepit *Buford*, an old troop ship.
The men go into steerage, already cold. No doctor says, "cough."
Metal bunks. Straw mattresses. Two basins to vomit in. That's
    Hoover in the launch, yelling,
      "Merry Christmas!" You thumb your nose.

You sleep all day. No vigilantes rush into your cabin,
    twisting the testicles of lovers. No dreams
of auditoriums, your cheeks flushed, men in the front row,
looking up, gleaming like wet stones. Why is this room damp?
    The ground without trees? You stumble to the door.
    He's young enough to bow, the soldier

grabbing your arm, following you to the toilet. Twelve hours?
You're that far away from yourself, New York, decency. You demand
    to talk with the men. "Impossible." But Sasha's
    let up, to tell you about thin blankets, leaky
bulkheads, salt water for washing, the lack of soap, threadbare
towels. The guards think you shot McKinley. Bombed the local
    church. Sasha bends over with cramps,
    stiffens in his steps, while they ask about
dynamite, anarchist crimes. Now your men are singing old songs,
in a language that hardens beyond recall, that congeals the tongue,
    breaking off like taffy.
    Where will you not be a stranger?

January. The English Channel. An Allied destroyer in your narrow
    wake. There's no bread, before the North Sea,
drifting and forgotten mines. Badly listing, you slip through
the Kiel Canal; stop for repairs. Men locked below are crumpling
    notes for the German workers, tossing out
    news, while sledges thunder on the hull.
Welders pull away in boats, singing of revolution. *Matushka Rossiya!*
You, Red Emma, can't remember the Russian for "bowl," "pencil,"
    "breast." Have you reversed the tilt of your
    womb? Lovers left you for children; left you
on platforms, sweating, as police roared up the aisles, clubbing
words back into mouths, shackling men who would not go to war.
    Now the *Buford* can't dock at Libau.
    The White Army's fighting to the death; the Baltic
crowded with blood, blockade, intervention. The engine pounds.
Shudders. Halts. You hear the flat, feverish cries of men
    with daughters in Chicago, their frozen
    breath shattered in midair.

Finland. Safety. At Hango, you get provisions to live on
    three days. Bayonets poke you

toward the train, soldiers open your packages, bundles, helping
themselves to scarfs and cheese. Sasha lines up the men,
    dear friend, even here, at blocked
    exits, he finds air at the hinge of every
door. The Americans, their ship, the young soldiers, fade
like wind-blown fog over miles of ice, a thickened harbor
    closing behind them. A stern lieutenant
    says, "Speeches will not do here." In what
idiom do you answer? You can barely speak, after thirty-five
years: government's paunchy, red-eyed jailers; the matrons who cut
    your ration; clerks with ink-stained fingers
    tucking money under blotters, pointing always
to the curve of sky, where light disappears. You send telegrams
to the People's Commissars. Wrench a last scarf out of dirty hands.
    Soon you'll be home. There'll be Feinberg.
    Gorki's wife. Kisses that do not penetrate.

Workers and peasants surround you at the border: eyes glowing
    in dark recesses. Music. Song. You are welcome
here, the American felon, the daughter returned, weeping
on the road to Petrograd. Sasha's sick; solitude breaking loose
    in his lungs. Zorin takes you
    in his car through quiet streets, the snow clean
in headlights. Sudden forms. Bright circles in the eyes. Hands.
"Propusk!" Zorin produces his pass. Rifles wave him on. Was there
    a revolution? You stay in the Astoria Hotel;
    others in the Smolny, school for aristocrats.
Zorin's wife, pregnant, lays out herring and kasha, moving in and out
of shadow, tall against the larder. She talks of hunger, created
    by the compassionate West. The old guard's armies
    that scar Russia; Denikin, Kolchak, Yudenich
spilling blood of new-born consciousness. Strong backs needed now.
Harsh ways. Glittering squads at dawn. Trunks filled with *propuski.*
    No one worse than your own intelligentsia.
    Sasha keeps asking: "Who is this 'it'?"

Days of talk. Old friends, like Bill Shatoff, bulging in the cold
      with open arms. At the anarchists' meeting,
you hear of the Cheka. Machine guns. Bolsheviks seizing food
and fuel. Not everyone speaks at the Petro-Soviet. Long queues
      for wormy cereal, frozen potatoes,
      bloated blue prostitutes tugging the sleeves
of Red soldiers. It's the blockade, Zorin says. Counter-revolution.
The flabby Zinoviev agrees, his voice cracking like an adolescent's.
      You nurse Sasha, break his fever; speak
      soothingly into the night. Zorin's wife
laughs at the offer of infant clothes. You, pampered *bourgeoisie*,
remember how Papa beat you in Königsberg. Now, the Party rules
      with *rastrellyat*, bullet-chipped walls. The people
      are stupid. Dark. Brutal. One beats them back,
Lenin's wolf at their throats. Only the indignant labels change,
like *Defiance*, the clothes you made in prison, listening to Missouri
      accents. Night-sounds. Rumbling trucks. You
      pull the covers to Sasha's chin, shivering yourself.

Marie Curie at the Grand Canyon
1921

Poor Mrs. Meloney, too, has collapsed, unable to come
      this far: the train rocking
      three days through the sandy heart
of America. A crowd's crushing handshake. Arm in a sling.
You're afraid to look down from the hotel window,
      your daughters riding the crest,
      stiff on Indian ponies, in awe
of such striated depths. They shriek. And joy is echoless
in the spaces around you. Objects guessed at. Each day,
      cataracts draping a darker
      gray between feelings and broken
horizon. The President praised your "radioactive heart,"
giving America's gift (not the radium, but the lead casket,
      locked; the real gram
      glowing in a vault): as if a friend
had died at sea, the small light a phosphorescent ash
of spurious bones; the gowned women applauding in ballrooms.

Pierre used to display the vial at dinner, its blue
      pulsing in the dark, his hand,
      a silhouette in the mist
surrounding his voice, holding up the salt that burns,
that turns the back of the hand violet in casual
      encounter. (Was he touching
      the pocket over his heart,
when the carriage ran him down? You stroked his soiled clothes,
kissed the strips of cloth your sister flung into the fire.)
      Close to the edge, and not: Mrs. Meloney,
      gray-haired, gray-faced, limping into receptions,

announcing the surrogates, Irene and Eve, while you rested.
Reporters ask about Carpentier and Dempsey, but the battle
       is aching joints; thin blood;
        breath that draws off like the slightest
fume. Always in black, you move like shadow into shadows,
vaguely luminous, hands transparent, fingertips peeling.

You want nothing for yourself. There must be radium.
      Voltmeters. Flasks. Separators.
      Lead shields. You know how much hot
distillation is in Baltimore, Denver, New York,
the drops flung off America's heaps of carnotite,
       tons pulverized in Pittsburgh,
       while you move through crowds,
"Benefactress of the Human Race." (Someone at the station
whispered, "Go home." How many Americans died in France?)
       "There will be more children
      of our children." Perhaps Irene will
win a Nobel: always doing, at your elbow. Years ago,
following you in the Renault, jolting behind trenches,
       eluding the gas, taking X-rays,
       penetrating the skin of war. You've come
for her future. It sways, when you move: the gold key
on a silken cord, Harding's key, hanging heavy on your neck.

Michael Collins Ambushed by Republicans
on the Road to Bealnamblath

1922

It comes. A quick knock above the right ear;
darkness entering a flap in the skull, dissolving the tongue.
His coat open, like the car he's fallen out of; hair black across
    his brow; a face recently made sanguine
    by pints of Wrastler, draining the August
twilight. The memory of the road twists through a gap in flowers,
there, into the rising mist, the man waving him to Bandon, rifles
    cracking in the woods, clipping leaves,
    the armored car clanking, McPeake
asking which way. He's slumped into that noise, voices
like men in the burning hotel, Cathal Brugha shooting with both hands.
    O'Connell's leaning above him, praying,
    heartily sorry. No one can see the far sun
kissing shut his eyes; hear him call his old father, scattering
seed into the wind, walking the fields, open-palmed and free.
    There's time in the closing of a father's
    grasp. It's another prison he's entering,

    within rage, the soft heart: silence
released like petals, O'Connell's voice stripped to a stem;
a kind of humming in his left ear opening like a throat.
    He can't recite O'Connell's
    sorrow and offense, feel the wet hand
behind his head. Everything translucent now: he's stroking
the air like a swimmer, the heatless flame sealing the backs
    of his eyes, where the plow
    digs furrows on father's land, the rented acres
he's dying for, dirt filling his shoes, the Cork women wailing
in back rooms. He's the stranger at every scene: doors like glass,

through which he sees O'Reilly
and Dalton, heads bowed, the table stained
with stout, bottles on the floor, someone's Webley broken open,
cartridges scattered like dead insects. Will he breathe
    niter? A texture of
    lace dragged across the tongue, fingernails

    splitting to the quick, without pain, jagged
corners of light crumbling in his lungs, where fluid seeps
like sea on the North Wall. All boats empty, he's reflected
    in the Liffey, waving at himself;
    a girl, with dress blown against her long body,
stepping into a bayonet. Now he's on the speaker's platform, raising
his fist. The crowd does not applaud. Wind blows through workmen,
    dust through shadows. It's all happening
    somewhere: a rebel sitting in the chair, tied back,
his gangrened leg stinking up Kilmainham yard. He lifts his face
into bullets. There's no plank bed here; no candlesticks on a rough
    table. The soiled blankets are leaves
    mulching the bones of the seasons, turning
under the droppings of birds. He's now not even a name, drifting
above rifle smoke. Something's hauled into the car, the mist heavy
    in all of Cork; no one weeping
    while this uprising takes his breath away.

Marcus Garvey Arrested at the 125th Street Station
1925

Squat, overweight, he's preening
like a diplomat. Is hope a fraud, because one man
receives an empty envelope? The train moves on to Grand Central.
A bright manacle around his wrist; the fur collar of his overcoat
an open noose. Each
side, they crush him
into himself, into darkness of soul, the black light
like a wet flow of words, Black Cross nurses marching down
Lenox Avenue, memories
crowding like crayfish, mountain mullet,
the bats in Jamaica. Is he the boy with dust on his feet?
How many *darkies* complained to the Attorney General? There's
no good in quadroons, any
shade of white, captains who drink
in dry dock while the cargo rots. His people do not straighten
hair, bleach their skins: lined up at the dock, waving to the first
Negro freighter
that ever left these shores.

"I would rather die
than be good, if being good means
extermination." What's war? Black factories. Black land.
Ethiopia fulfilled. Europeans annihilating each other, wrong
color ants on a red
hill. Isn't he a great man?
DuBois raving at him, while he vows to be "the wreck of matter."
That defector, Eason, shot down in New Orleans; the KKK wordless,
sending someone a severed
hand; cousins to men in East St. Louis

who nailed boards over doors and windows, poured kerosene on porches,
burned black families alive. He needs more than corroded boilers
        to float an army
        from Biloxi, to navigate a sea
already crossed by the dead, to raise a profit from ashes.
He's been in their tombs before, seen their fat fists, heard
        in a crowded courtroom
        the click of a judge's false teeth.

        Heat escapes between such
    bars. Dampness freezes along doorjambs.
All jailers have jowls. Nothing worth counting in his
pockets: scraps of paper, notes from Amy, ticket stubs, folded
        blank stock
        for shares in boats
that sink in the Hudson. The nations league against him
in Geneva, while he's banned from Liberia, and men who confiscate
        his land
        receive medals from France.
In Liberty Hall, plumes waving in his admiral's hat,
he took away the mop and broom: cashed in a people's
        dream of black sunrise,
        black navies; the SS *Yarmouth*
steaming past Ellis Island. Must he roll all his fingers in ink,
to make a mark? He hears the desk sergeant sigh. Keys jangling.
        The match put to the *Negro World,*
        his plump shadow hissing into the sea.

Mohandas Gandhi Awakened by Flashlights
near the Sea

1930

Twin beams, fingers stabbing
at his face; two British officers asking
if he is himself, awakening now in the open air, women
gathering by the reed cottage, his few teeth suspended
like shards of pottery;
the mango grove here
at Dandi the last barrier and night forest, a rising
coolness, words half-spoken, dying in the throat. Last month
he waded into the sea,
his dhoti lifted
dry, homespun khadi gleaming white as the limestone buildings
of Porbandar, where he learned to walk, to read Gujarati words
drawn with a stick
on the floor of the dust school.
He's been waiting for this: having bent to sand, sifted through salt
left by the tide, breaking foreign laws against collecting blood's
need. Is there no profit in the sun?
His people pour the sea into shallow pans.

He asks to wash his face
and brush his teeth. The officers
look at their watches. "Hurry, please." Will he lead
the march against the Dharasana Salt Works? Someone else
rises; another;
another. "Please hurry up!"
He asks Pundit Khare to sing the Vaishnava hymn, the song of Rama.
On the ground, legs folded, Khare plucks the single string, every
Indian chanting.
The officers keep fidgeting

as Khare sings of the ideal husband, the ideal wife, names
the Redeemer. Who across the dark waters, in the streets of Durban,
         the Transvaal, or London,
            would weave
his body into such a trance? In the hills of Natal, on that other
continent, he'd given up stormy plungings of the groin, embracing
         brahmcharya, where Zulus pulled
            turbaned merchants in rickshaws.

         The followers, the resisters, bow
      to touch his feet. He has no message for
Kasturbai. "Tell her she is a brave girl." Have they not
known each other since children in marriage? She's been to Yeravda
         Jail, in Poona,
            bent to ahimsa, the nonviolence
of love. He will again refuse to eat: Churchill raging,
the mills closing in Lancashire; Indians spinning their own cotton,
         wearing Khaddar, as they give up
            alcohol and dirt, sell tiny bags of salt,
crowd the prisons. No General Dyer now, in Amritsar, blocking
exits, shooting them down. He remembers Johannesburg, when he washed
         the bodies of plague-infected
            men. The righteous do not ward off
blows. Will he come this way? They've brought three lorries
of police. No one speaks, as he waves his hand toward the shore,
         and nods;
            forbids all weeping.

Kaethe Kollwitz Installs Her Statues
at Roggevelde Cemetery
1932

Chains clash, swing free: the Mourning Mother left
        kneeling
         above you.
The Father, on his separate base, stiffly
withdrawn, while she curves forward, arms hugging
        herself,
        puckering
a shawl, eyes closed. Neither you nor she can
lift her face to the rows of white crosses,
        the anonymous young
        of 1914.
Does she meditate, listen to mist, grasp
the cry of gulls? You know the vacancy
        of her body,
        your son, Peter,
fallen at Diksmuide. His face blurs now,
   receding like the detail you omit
        in the black
        of woodcuts.

The Father, your granite husband: it's Karl,
        caught
        between piety
and anger, arms folded, like the foreman
watching men unload bricks at the Pregel
        River, near
        the dock. Why is he
praying in the barge? The line of his jaw
straightens a landscape. His arms, locked against

his lungs,
          almost prevent
breathing. You could make boundaries of his back.
He's the one from *Das Ende*, laying out
          stiff rebels
          in the Mill.
In the evenings, in your unlit room, you
know him home from clinic halls, the "Arzt," man
          with a
          damaged heart.

  The overhead birds, the incoming fog,
          the softening
          ground: one might
stay here, fill emptiness between trees, be
one's own monument. You stroke the gray cheek
          of a woman
          gone out
of you. This face belongs to art. Which one
looks back at evening? Karl knows, murmuring
          "yes, yes."
          You don't weep
alone. The day dissolves into raw stone.
You're somewhere else: Berlin. Your work hidden
          untitled
          behind curtains,
already out of favor, soon a crime.
At Güstrow, they'll pluck down Barlach's angel,
          the bronze
          copy of your eyes.

Things are finished here. Mother and Father
          will not
          unchain the space

between them. On this level ground, bodies
drift away, your hand moves out of nature,
            clay women
            bend
beneath the sculpted, swollen knuckles not
your own. At home, on the worktable, forms
            grow small,
            the reichsmark
immense. The air expands like a stomach
no one can fill. You see the birds leaving
            from a
            dark tower,
wings dipping downward in a stiff salute,
earth emptying itself of the damp breath
            of Roggevelde's
            dead.

Mao Tse-Tung at Pao An,
after the Long March
1935

Little Lin, bag of
bones, gives flowers
if you will not kill mother. Laughter rolls down the slope.
You come armed with speech, the Red Army a mist that captures
moonlight in a valley
where hands
break open sacks in a landlord's yamen. Here in the hills
one eats millet; people dance out of caves, as if being
liberated, showing off
sisters they won't
lose for taxes, waving banners and signs they can't read.
They keep coming, like beads from father's broken abacus,
pinched through
fingers, scattered in small graves, as old men stroke beards
and ask for opium.

Once, you dreamt
of Pang, millstone
maker, grinding your head: the Generalissimo grinning
in shadows beyond oil lamps, hand flashing with needle
and thread,
unable to mend
terror. You hear distant thunder. Or is it his planes?
Who unbinds the feet of women had a mother hobbling in
paddies. You swam
the lotus pond
of Shaoshan: thought of her wet hands and the sounds
in the sky like scrubbing stones, her Buddhist statues
rolling down the mountain.

Your wounded did not complain, shivering, sitting up, tied
                to trees when they slept in swamps.

                The Future
                is one's lost
personality: bruised from sleeping on a peasant's mat.
You reach for the wife executed in Changsha, always taste
                the missing
                tongue,
as children run down the loess hills, disappear into small
clefts. Who saves China follows a white goat's-hair rope
                through snow,
                he hears wooden
clappers, a rhythm like the throbbing in a toad's throat,
the vein in your temple. There will be evenings like this,
                clear and cold,
when you remember crossing the mountains, giving your coat
                to a dying stranger.

Antonin Artaud in the Land
of the Tarahumaras
1936

Twelve days he's begged the only official to allow
    Ciguri,
    the Peyote Dance,
the healing. And now the sorcerers come down
the mountain, the landscape of casual crucifixion
    where rocks are torn into
limbs and open mouths, women bent under the weight
    of mirrors and crosses,
the air heavy with the blood of his breathing.
From Antwerp to Havana to Vera Cruz, his body
    burning cold,
    bursting like a bubo,
deprived of opium. He must be clean
to receive the God, the failures of Paris
    digging a manicured
    nail into his sex.

He must be split open somewhere behind his reach,
    where the soul
    gapes, his name
loosens: childhood snapping in the wind
like a cloak, his life impaled, trembling,
    the goat's heart
on the stick of the sorcerer, who buries peyote
    in the hole
under the inverted bowl: the dome of life
shading the twisted figures of genitals,
    at the entrance
    to the circle of illness,

where birds fall dead and the unborn
rot in the womb. Enter, O enter! They've come,
      the magic ones,
        to suck Europe from his

organs. He drinks Teguino, the liquor, the searing
      fluid
        drained from his Being
as far back as Marseilles, when two pimps
stabbed him in the back. Was that the first emptiness?
      Three sorcerers mount a log,
riding it within the circle of the dance, calling him
      forth, scooping
his body hollow as a gourd. They grind peyote,
crushed male and female. He eats. Now the sacred
      spitting
        into a hole, deep
where nothing of his saliva may rise to light again,
where the sun's dark twin takes him into her mouth,
      Nanaqui, the boy he was,
      masticated,

baptized. Something sprinkled on his head. Rattles
      knocked against
      his brow, a sorcerer
leaving the circle to piss like a bull,
fart like thunder. What power of excrement
      brings the body
back? He was always elsewhere, listening for speech,
      the angel, the messenger,
whose touch fused the fragile bones of his tongue
when he stood up stammering. He goes deeper now,
      spits, staggers, falls
      into sleep. Like an embryo,

he floats on himself, lies back on the curve
of the earth, supine in the moment before dawn,
    when he must
     heal.

IV

Bruno Bettelheim at Dachau
1938

Run. Run. Inside the Jourhaus, they erase your name.
      The nearest face blurs
      into a voice, shrieking
you cannot replace your broken glasses here.
You can't see the sleeve of the new man you are.
      In the distance of rattling
      cattle cars, a sudden engine
takes away your breath, grizzled men sneer.
A tyro, your number is too high. They tell you
      about the old days,
      when the smart ones died.
Ten miles from Munich? Earth's end seemed further
toward darkness, the edge of a Polar sea, beyond
      habitation. Your head aches.
      You're bleeding from your
side. If you faint, they will carry you off,
into the space between trees, their final empire.

The guard tells you to pick up the pebble,
      bring it
      rolling to his palm.
It's the wrong one. Older prisoners stare at dirt
lodged under fingernails. If the rifle butt comes
      down, you'll never again
      tie a string: child, fumbling
with shoelaces, despised like the man eating grass,
"Moslem" in filth. Will another pebble change you?
      Will there be a Bettelheim
      using "I,"

awakening in a different skin, rushing out at 4 a.m.,
when sirens scream for the peeling away of self?
  He laughs, walking away,
  only a boy
talking of your castration. In prison, a man
spits on his neighbor, reviles his God, slaps his friend.

Here's the Kapo. Jew beating Jews. You face the wall
  like a dunce, you become
  invisible. You can't ask the enemy
why he assists the enemy. You quiz a failing memory:
name the town you come from, the school, who wrote
  the last letter,
  quoting someone who quoted
you. There's a middle-class man weeping
because they do not call him "Herr." Is there
  status on the dung
  hill? The SS marches
through, where frail men stare at stones
like autistic children. Others are waving flags,
  tightening armbands,
  jealous brothers
complaining to father. You walk, to find out
what a man's born to be, curving to the shape of a blow.

Three weeks. Not three years. You're still alive.
  The guard shoots
  over the flat row of straw beds.
Nothing nicked. It's a good job. You can get on line
for coffee. In winter, they let you sleep
  until the farm animals
  yawn, and stir,
standing in stalls, stained by their own urine.
Are they driven out five abreast? The guard is pointing

to your number.
He's taking you
to the Jourhaus, for release, smiling. Finally,
you've been recognized, paid for, lifted dripping
from a sewer. But he brings you
back. Oh some mistake
on your part, having hope. A truncheon prods body
to the limit. The spirit snaps like a small stick.

Starvation edema. Cheeks swollen. Eyes glittering.
The orchestra of ragged men
had brass violins
in your dream. And he's done it, the man
who promised to hang himself. How does one hold on?
You'll always sleep
curled into a ball.
This one clutches a crust of bread. He calls women,
and whimpers, and masturbates, with no resul..
There's nothing special
about dying. Why do the new ones
talk of escape? The Kapo ladles soup from the top
if you're stupid. Your blood's thin as an old woman's,
whispering in your ears,
the mind a bowl
filling with images. You lift something to the light
like the rumor of a double ration of bread. An idea.

Record. Remember. It's what the child you took into your
home could not feel
in his clenched fist.
He arrived without a name to turn to, almost without
a skin, a surface to touch. You taught him textures
of food, the point of a pin,
the arc of an encircling arm.

Did he remain numb to spite your goodness? When
does the tongue taste sand? Only new prisoners talk
      of humiliation. War.
      Think, rather, what vegetable's
in the soup. How the guard knocks men with glasses
into the latrine pit, calling them "asshole,"
      while the Brick Commando
      trots past. How the Commandant,
impersonal as a photograph, standing in the compound
back of his home, peers through a hole in your chest.

Eugene O'Neill at Tao House
1941

He wakes sweating from a dream of fog.
It's here: the cough, the rattle of the lunger, flophouse
salute; something long gone in the kidneys. Ship's bells.
  Yesterday, words spiraled
 across the page, out of reach, his hands
trembling. In his study, in the porthole light, it's 1912:
a lost tide washing down blank paper like watered whiskey.
  He'll shrive them all:
 mother, dazed as ever, gesturing
like St. Francis at birds never there. He hears
Jamie's greeting from the clipped shrub, the woody thing
  that grows even in death, his brother
grinning; sweat pouring from wastrel's chin into collarless
shirt. Their words begin to blur. Black out. Like the bulbs
  father said, burning, would put him in the poorhouse.
The last play? Whatever flame he sinks into now, from which he
  came, burns away the voice, consumes cathedrals.

  Each day's silence, like the war, a thin
cloud settling on walnut trees; sun disappearing into
long grasses on Mount Diablo. Carlotta's hidden the house
  in its white walls;
 "Keep Out" signs blocking the mile-long
road; wrought iron twisted on the gate, ancient symbols
spelling out "The Way." She types scenario, dialogue,
  using her magnifier,
 his script so small it's almost flattened
to her palm; still the actress she was in photos, posing
in the Grecian manner, head against his cheek, both of them

facing a distant sky, the shrinking
gods. How he misses the sea. It's easy to navigate dry
between colored mirrors, teakwood dragons, Chinese Chippendale,
      Coromandel screen; everything from
Gump's edge of the world, an hour's drive, the city intact.
      Shop windows crackling in the moon's wake.

      Like Hickey in Hope's saloon, he bullies
dreaming spirits to drive them out of doors, keeps dropping
the pencil. Coffee spills on his sleeve, brown swill, words
            sinking beneath unsteady
      hands, like the keys of a player piano.
"You should have nothing else to do," Carlotta says. "Just
write." And closes the blinds, her eyes in pain from sunlight,
            too used to the semidark.
      Shane's coming for a visit, the son
draining him like alimony, who wants to raise horses in Colorado.
"Let him scrub decks on a ship. *My* father kept me on the dole."
      That night, his legs twitch, he tries to run,
and wakes, remembering the house on Peaked Hill Bar sliding
into the sea. Do parents ever love more than themselves? Sudden
      wind in the valley. Who'll feed him, when the spoon
falls? At Jimmy the Priest's, he rose from the cot like Lazarus,
      vomiting Veronal and five-cent whiskey.

      He's weak, following the brick path in back
that winds upon itself; standing in the new pool, looking
over the tiles, down the mountain. There's Blemie, his old
            Dalmatian, taking the sun,
      chipmunks tearing across the lawn, Carlotta
pink against the peach groves, fidgeting with her blouse
and hair, hands suited to music, contemptuous as glass.
            All writing washed away
      at Dunkirk: gone, the world's drowse; gone,

the road to Le Plessis, rented chateau, where his Electra
listened to her ghosts. Everything sinks far away. Poland.
     Finland. France. Radio news: his silence.
This, too, is history, a man speaking into his private dark.
In the core of his bones, a tremor; knees knocking; the earth
     heaved up in fire. The British are mining
the sea lanes of Singapore, while Carlotta waves, Blemie struggles
     to his feet; not even clouds darken the valley.

Ezra Pound in the Cage,
near Pisa
1945

No one's dead on death row. No one speaks to the green
        look of his
        eyes: oxen
swaying past the outdoor cages, on the road to Viareggio,
sun imprinting x's on his face, the shadows of a vengeful
        web.
        He hears
a kind of chatter going from cage to cage, questions about
the Bible: American speech, lost recitations carried away
        by the birds
        who sit on wires
like musical notes. Is this man a tympanist, thumping a
bucket? It's the honey man, collecting turds like names.
        Much thanks!
        No one goes
deaf or mad, deprived of belt, shoelaces: pants sagging,
tongue flapping on the instep. They'll never hang a poet
        with a mouth so dry of song.

His tarpaper roof, a black page between head and heaven,
        as four
        mental cases
run for the fence, draped there, riddled by men in towers.
All night the spotlights wake condemned sleepers, as if
        to find
        a ram's blood
for speakers in Hades. At Aversa, certain throats will be
too small: crushed larynx, lips stained with language

                      one tries
                      to record.
Is he the worst offender? Reinforced bars, electrified
trees: no Fascist commando will save him. The eyes burn
                      to read
                      the rules
against decency. This solitude inflames the passageway
between voice and ear. Noon dust penetrates the skin.
                      He believes in weather:

clear night chill flowing through wire mesh, a silver
                      light not
                      the moon over Taishan.
Yesterday he watched a wasp getting born, slipping into
the world, green against green. When he sloughs the six
                      blankets
                      he's gray
against gray stone. How many ways to pitch a voice, call
to heaven with a broken oath, while a darkening roof lowers
                      to his thin
                      crown? Is it
madness not to breathe? Where's Dorothy? Where's Olga?
The crickets are rubbing something on the sweet nerve of
                      silence.
                      He hears
shoveling behind the tents, the escaped dead shuffling home,
hands filling x's with plaster the way they filled his mouth
                      with bad words on Rome radio.

Georgia O'Keeffe Takes Over the Old
Hacienda in Abiquiu, New Mexico
1945

If rattlesnakes have odor, that's it, dry and sweet.
        No taut length
        of electric wire
above the arroyo. Moon. Candles. Hills like swellings
beneath clouds, folding into sutures. Vision itself a wound,
        always healing.
        On the roof, she thumbs
light; the heaved, sea-bed mesa, fixed and primordial,
though it changes in the movement of her shadow. A studio
        must be blank, the back
        of a hand that never touched
pigs, cattle, with the tough fibers of her grip. Workman's
sledge driving now into the crumbling adobe wall, making
        a square of space she will fit
        with glass, framing the valley,
the green line of crops. Decoration on wooden tables?
Antelope skull. Pelvis. Orifice through which color sings.

    She writes Stieglitz every day. Husband. Aging friend,
        resting on his cot
        in back of an American Place,
heart failing like his reputation. Her spelling still bad.
Sudden wind exhales topsoil, whistles past Penitente *moradas,*
        old crucifix. Was that his last
        breath? The doorway's dark space
in the patio wall: an emptiness in the middle of hardened
thought. She can still hear his words swirl and flourish
        like a cape. But she's
        too old for fathers.

The long barns of Lake George too empty of feeling.
He'd criticize things here. The flower unseemly,
       floating behind the eye
       of a skull, the pale blue curve,
black on black. Ice cream now. Affection. His needs
thinning out, like his white hair, parting in a breeze.

  All supplies going to Los Alamos, the Government,
       she lacks nails
       and boards. For plaster,
women stroke wet earth on the walls, smoothing contours
pink, as if in the nude. They are like water on petals,
       moving into horn
       and valley where pollen
slides along the stamen. She can see the old church.
Each room with its fireplace, the light at times easy
       to penetrate as mountain
       air, but no looking down
at factories along the East River, no Radiator Building
blocking the sun. Plenty of height in her spine, charcoal
       smooth as the moon's
       curve on flattened paper.
In the whiteness of bone, eye socket, broken shank, she's
the student of nuns, scooping remains of desert flowers.

J. Robert Oppenheimer at Alamogordo
1945

The Test suspended: sudden rain sweeping the plateau
   named for birds,
   arroyos
awash with mating toads. He can stop brushing teeth
with cola and sweet blood, stop plotting world's end
   in prefabs, block
   houses, his camp
running mud from barbed wire down to a rickety bridge.
It's up there in the tower's tin shack riding the wind,
   looped cables
   spilling like intestines.
A novel's been left on its blunt nose, pages folded at
everyday lust. The prism of its heart yet untouched.
   Is this what the land
   requires?
(Remember the sloop, *Trimethy,* tacking into a tidal rush
against the odds on Great South Bay?) He smokes, coughing.
   Gullies froth with scum, insect husks.

Two mornings ago, someone screamed, pointing at Venus,
   the near light
   at which he laughed,
cigarette burning to his lips like a fuse. Apache
saw a white star falling here. How many pilots saw it
   before the bombers
   moaned through
on night runs? The toads throb in foxholes, desiring.
He warns everyone to use welder's glass over the eyes,
   hide behind yuccas,
   turn away.

It's time to fill the sacs behind fangs, ignite a black
star in the pit of the stomach. The Test is really on.
                    No American town
                    will turn to bone.
Fermi shreds paper to throw like confetti in the face of air,
to measure blow-by, to crow triumphant before Kisty's needles,
            to leap above panicles of cactus flowers.

The rain pulls up into itself, caught in a backward magnetic
                    field: crackling voices
                    like cabbies in Santa Fe
competing toward dawn. How much can a man be counted on?
Rattler under rock, lizard, scorpion, little here to save.
                    (No fear of lone
                    aircraft, persimmon
snapped at levels of the horse's mouth. No taro-leaf shade.
At epicenter, women see a blue light, hear only the rush of
                    cloth: silken
                    skin hung in flaps,
bridges bent like licorice.) He hears the dream chatter
of Urakami's crickets, wings and leaves blackening on wind,
                    turbid song of
                    toads in darkness.
One hand flayed by alkali of desert water, he comprehends
flow. And turns away, crouched before a burning tree, trying
            to believe in evil.

Notes

Roald Amundsen (1872–1928?)

Amundsen, of course, reached the South Pole before the British party led by Robert Falcon Scott. Scott and his men, after finding evidence of Amundsen's arrival at the Pole, froze to death on their way back to base camp.

Amundsen died years later in a plane crash in the Arctic Ocean, on his way to rescue his friend Umberto Nobile, whose dirigible had crashed near Spitsbergen, a group of islands north of Norway.

Antonin Artaud (1896–1948)

In May 1935, the production of Artaud's play *Les Cenci* failed with the critics. Artaud despaired of ever having his ideas on the Theatre of Cruelty understood in Europe. He went to Mexico in search of vital forces for renewal.

Bruno Bettelheim (b. 1903)

Before his arrest in the spring of 1938, Dr. Bettelheim had taken an autistic child into his home. From 1938 until his release in 1939, Dr. Bettelheim was imprisoned first at Dachau, then at Buchenwald.

Michael Collins (1890–1922)

Along with Eamon de Valera and Arthur Griffith, Michael Collins was a key figure in the Irish struggle against Britain that led to the treaty of 1921. Although Collins had become a national hero in his work with the Irish Volunteers and the Irish Republican Army, once he signed the treaty that partitioned Ireland and required an oath of allegiance to the crown, Collins was seen by De Valera and IRA insurgents as having sold out to the British. Civil War ensued, after Griffith became president of the provisional government of the new Irish Free State and Collins head of the army. When Griffith died of a stroke on August 12, 1922, Collins became head of the government. He was killed ten days later during a military inspection tour.

Crazy Horse (1842?–77)

The quoted phrase in the title of the poem is taken from Mari Sandoz's biography, *Crazy Horse: The Strange Man of the Oglalas*.

In 1874, gold was discovered in the Black Hills (Pa Sapa), a territory sacred to all the Dakotas, and rumors were spreading that soon Custer would be leading a force into the area. Crazy Horse learned of his daughter's death (caused or preceded by the "white man's cough") after returning from leading a small war party against the Crow Indians. By himself, using directions from his people, he went in search of her death-scaffold.

Two years later occurred the great battle at Little Big Horn between Custer and the combined forces of the Dakotas and Cheyenne.

"Loafer" was the name apparently given to an Indian who had grown too dependent on the white man, living on a reservation or near a fort.

"Hunkpatila" is the name of a group within the Oglala tribe, of which Crazy Horse was a member.

Marie Curie (1867–1934)

To assist Madame Curie in her research, Marie Meloney, a journalist, raised money through public subscription to buy a gram of radium and have it given as a gift from the United States. She then organized Madame Curie's visit.

Fyodor Dostoevsky (1821–81)

In April 1849, members of conversation groups that met at the houses of Mikhail Petrashevsky and Sergey Durov were arrested by the Tzarist police. Their crime was that they discussed ways of changing, if not overthrowing, the Tzarist state. Around April 14, Dostoevsky had been invited to read aloud two letters to the Petrashevsky group. One letter had been written by the novelist Nikolai Gogol to the critic Visarrion Belinsky, reproving Belinsky for his review of Gogol's *Selected Passages from Correspondences with My Friends*. Belinsky, while dying of consumption, wrote a massive rejoinder of over twenty pages, viciously attacking Gogol and the

Tzar's government. For reading the Belinsky letter, and for making hand-written copies of it and preparing to print it, Dostoevsky was arrested, im-prisoned for eight months in the Peter and Paul Fortress, where he was interrogated, and then in December 1849 taken to Semyonov Square, at which place he heard himself sentenced to death.

The evening before his arrest, Dostoevsky had been caught in a sudden rainstorm. He stopped off at the home of his friend Dr. Stephen Yanovsky to change his clothes and borrow money. Yanovsky had no money, but he did lend Dostoevsky one of his suits.

Dostoevsky's mother died in 1837, when Dostoevsky was sixteen. One of the few things he kept from her was a medallion inscribed with the motto,

> *J'ai le coeur tout plein d'amour,*
> *Quand l'aurez-vous à votre tour?*

He carried the medallion with him all his life.

A little more than two years after Dostoevsky's mother died, his father, who had been a physician at the Hospital of the Poor in Moscow, was brutally murdered by peasants.

Frederick Douglass (1817–95)

According to his own account, Douglass was accompanied on the speakers' platform in Tremont Temple by the Hon. Thomas Russell, Miss Anna E. Dickinson, Rev. Mr. Grimes, J. Sella Martin, and William Wells Brown.

John Brown tried to enlist Douglass's help for his raid on Harpers Ferry. When Brown was captured, Douglass, afraid of reprisals against himself, went to England. Annie, his favorite child, died while he was there.

Anna Douglass, though free when Douglass met her (he was still a slave), could not read or write.

Julia Griffiths arrived from England with money to help Douglass found his newspaper, *The North Star*. For a time, she lived in the Douglass home in Rochester.

Mohandas Gandhi (1869–1948)

In 1930, Gandhi launched the Salt Satyagraha to protest the British salt laws, under which the British controlled the means of producing salt while also levying a sales tax on it. Indians were forbidden to make their own salt or to buy it from anyone outside official government sources. In March, Gandhi, with a group of his followers and press correspondents, departed from his Sabarmati Ashram and led a two-hundred-mile march south to the coastal town of Dandi. There, in April, he publicly broke the law by gathering salt on the beach. The authorities finally arrested him on May 5.

The British also required Indians to send their raw cotton to England. Finished textiles were produced by mills in Lancashire and sold to India.

In India, during Gandhi's childhood, rural schools had no blackboards or books, and lessons were drawn on the dirt floor with sticks. They were known as dust schools.

Marcus Garvey (1887–1940)

Founder of the Universal Negro Improvement Association, Garvey came to the United States from Jamaica in 1916. From his headquarters in Harlem, he advocated black capitalism and established the Negro Factories Corporation and the Black Star Line. His business practices, however, were slipshod, and in 1923 he was convicted of mail fraud. In February 1925, his last appeal concerning his conviction was rejected. On his way back from Chicago, he was seized by Federal marshals at the 125th Street station.

He served two years of a five-year sentence and was deported in 1927.

Emma Goldman (1869–1940)

Both Emma Goldman and her friend Alexander Berkman had been imprisoned in 1917 in connection with their antidraft activities. Berkman, known as "Sasha," served his time in the Federal penitentiary in Atlanta, while Goldman was incarcerated at the Federal prison in Jefferson City, Missouri, where she helped make clothing.

Mitchell Palmer was the Attorney General of the United States, very busy deporting radicals, anarchists, etc. His work was assisted by the information-gathering talents of a recent employee of the Library of Congress, J. Edgar Hoover.

In 1919, unexploded mines from the World War made travel in the North Sea hazardous. Russia was being torn apart by civil war, while the Western countries, including the United States, blockaded its ports and tried to starve the Bolsheviks into submission.

D. W. Griffith (1875–1948)

A native of Kentucky, Griffith was only seven when his father, a former colonel in the Confederate army, died and left the family impoverished.

While Griffith was filming *The Birth of a Nation,* the World War broke out in Europe.

It is widely believed that *The Birth of a Nation,* originally titled *The Clansman,* after the novel by Thomas Dixon on which it was based, contributed to the activities of the Ku Klux Klan after the film's first appearance in 1915.

Kaethe Kollwitz (1867–1945)

Known primarily as a graphic artist, Kollwitz turned to sculpture as well after 1910. For eighteen years, following the death of her son, Peter, in an early battle of the World War, Kollwitz tried to design an appropriate monument to him. By 1932 she had eliminated Peter from the design and represented only the bereaved parents, modeled after herself and her husband, Karl, who was a physician. Later, in 1942, Kollwitz's grandson, named for her lost son, Peter, was killed at the Russian front.

In 1898, Kollwitz completed a series of six etchings, *Die Weber (The Weavers),* based in part on Hauptmann's drama of the same name, which depicted the unsuccessful weavers' revolt in Silesia in 1844. *Das Ende* is the last print in the series and reveals a workroom into which weavers killed in the revolt are being carried and laid out near a loom. Such work, with its strong social comment, made Kollwitz as unpopular with the Kaiser as she would later be with Hitler.

Ernst Barlach used Kaethe Kollwitz's face as the model for his *Hovering Angel,* the war memorial in Güstrow Cathedral destroyed by the Nazis. A casting of the angel may be seen in the Museum of Modern Art in New York.

Mao Tse-tung (1893–1976)

In October 1934, Mao led a force of 85,000 soldiers out of Kiangsi, in southeastern China, west to Yunnan, then north to Pao An, where he arrived in October 1935. Throughout this journey of 6,000 miles, Mao's troops were pursued and harassed by the Kuomintang armies of Chiang Kai-shek. Fewer than 20,000 survivors, the ragtag nucleus of the Red Army, made it to Pao An. This year-long experience of Mao and his troops is referred to as The Long March.

William Morris (1834–96)

Morris made two trips to Iceland, in 1871 and 1873, by which time he was an established poet, designer, and craftsman. In 1871, he took possession of the manor house of Kelmscott, in Oxfordshire, sharing it with his old friend, the painter and poet Dante Gabriel Rossetti (1828–82). By this time, Rossetti and Morris's wife, Jane, were deeply involved with each other. By 1880, however, that relationship was effectively over, though the dying Rossetti continued to write to Jane.

"Dante's / wife jailed above the marshes of Maremma" refers to a painting by Rossetti, *La Pia de' Tolomei,* which he began in 1868 and completed in 1880. The subject of the painting is taken from the fifth canto of Dante's "Purgatorio," in which Dante is approached by the spirit of Pia de' Tolomei, who had been murdered by her husband, but first imprisoned by him in a fortress of the Maremma, a coastal region in central Italy. The portrait shows a woman impassive, resigned, while behind her, through the window of her prison, one can see the marshes (sketches of which had been supplied to Rossetti by Fairfax Murray). Next to La Pia are a breviary, a rosary, and a packet of letters written by her husband when he was her lover. The model for this painting was Jane Morris.

The source for the raw detail on the 1880 trip up the Thames is Morris's unpublished manuscript in the British Library: "Description of an expedition by boat from Kelmscott House, Upper Mall, Hammersmith, to Kelmscott Manor, Lechlade, Oxfordshire, with critical notes."

The poem deals with Morris in the period just before he became a social activist.

Anna O (Bertha Pappenheim) (1859–1936)

After Dr. Breuer thought he had cured Bertha Pappenheim, he was summoned by her family to find her writhing in bed with an hysterical pregnancy. She was naming him as the father. In great distress, he was forced to abandon her case. After a mysteriously poorly documented period in Switzerland, where she was a mental patient, Ms. Pappenheim appeared to be in perfect health, and became a leading feminist and pioneer social worker.

Georgia O'Keeffe (b. 1887)

For some time, Georgia O'Keeffe had been spending a portion of every year in New Mexico, leaving Alfred Stieglitz (1864–1946), her husband, in New York.

Eugene O'Neill (1888–1953)

The O'Neills had a home with Chinese motifs built in the mountains near San Francisco. It was here that O'Neill wrote *Long Day's Journey into Night,* while struggling with the familial tremor that would soon make writing physically impossible. Carlotta, his wife, had installed a player piano in "Rosie's Room," a kind of den that contained fixtures from a saloon and memorabilia of Eugene's father, the actor James O'Neill.

J. Robert Oppenheimer (1904–67)

The testing of the first atomic bomb was almost delayed because of a rainstorm.

"Kisty" was the nickname for George Kistiakowski, the Russian-born chemist responsible for designing the triggering mechanism of the bomb.

Ezra Pound (1885–1972)

Pound had been living in the same household with both his wife, Dorothy Pound, and his mistress, Olga Rudge, before he surrendered to the U.S. Army. His anti-American remarks in broadcasts over Italian radio caused him to be accused of treason. Some of the men he was imprisoned with were accused of murder and were hanged at Aversa.

Marcel Proust (1871–1922)

In March 1914, Proust's beloved chauffeur, Alfred Agostinelli, enrolled in a flying school under the name of Marcel Swann. During a training flight, he crashed into the sea and drowned.

George Sand (1804–76)

George Sand's last long-term liaison was with Alexandre Manceau, an engraver fourteen years her junior, who became her devoted secretary. After years of jealous conflict, Sand's son, Maurice, demanded that she choose between himself and Manceau. Sand chose Manceau, leaving the estate home at Nohant, near the town of La Châtre, to be inhabited by Maurice and his wife.

In a little country house in Palaiseau, south of Paris, Sand lived with and nursed Manceau, who was dying of tuberculosis. She had already established a relationship with the plump painter Charles Marchal, her *dernier amour*.

Marie Dorval was a popular romantic actress with whom Sand probably had an affair. At the very least, they were dear friends. In her later years,

Dorval could not attract much of an audience. After her death in 1849 (the year that Chopin died), her grandchildren were taken care of by Sand.

In 1830, Aurore Dupin Dudevant (George Sand's real name) reached an agreement with her philandering husband, Casimir Dudevant, that she would live part of the year in Paris away from him, and part in Nohant. In Paris, she shared a garret with her lover, the young Jules Sandeau. In collaboration with Sandeau, Aurore Dudevant wrote novelettes under the name of J. Sand. By 1832, she was writing everything herself and was known as George Sand.

Orville Wright (1871–1948) and Wilbur Wright (1867–1912)

During his senior year in high school, and just before he was to begin study for the ministry, Wilbur Wright was struck in the mouth by a stick in a hockey game. While his mouth healed, and he was fitted with false teeth, Wilbur lived many months as a semi-invalid and recluse, developing stomach and heart trouble, drawn out of himself only by the needs of his dying mother.

New Directions Paperbooks—A Partial Listing

For complete listing request complete catalog from
New Directions, 80 Eighth Avenue, New York 10011   † Bilingual